Scott Foresman

Fresh Reads
for Fluency and Comprehension

Glenview, Illinois • Boston, Massachusetts • Chandler, Arizona • Upper Saddle River, New Jersey

ISBN 13: 978-0-328-48893-3
ISBN 10:   0-328-48893-3
10 V0N4 18 17 16 15 14 13

Contents

Name _______________________________

Look at the pictures. Then answer the questions that follow.

The First Day

Turn the page.

Fresh Reads   Unit R Week 1 SI

1 **How did the boy feel *before* he got on the bus?**

○ scared

○ happy

○ sleepy

2 **How did the boy's mother feel at the *beginning* of the story?**

○ angry

○ happy

○ worried

3 **Where was the boy going?**

○ to a park

○ to school

○ home

4 **Draw or write about how the boy felt *after* he got off the bus.**

Name ______________________________

Look at the pictures. Then answer the questions that follow.

Pam Skates

1

2

3

4

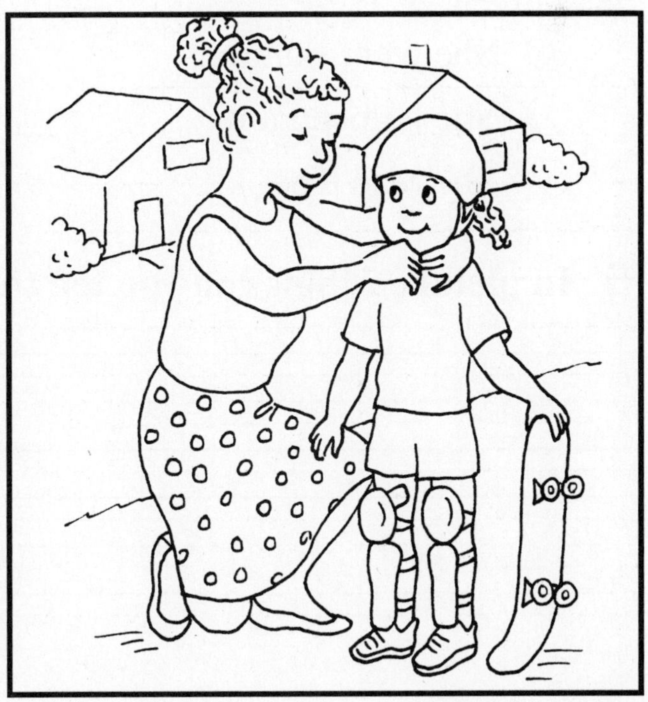

Turn the page.

Fresh Reads   Unit R   Week 1   OL

3

Answer the questions below.

1 **How did Pam feel in picture 1?**

- ○ scared
- ○ happy
- ○ angry

2 **What did Pam like to do?**

- ○ skate
- ○ jump rope
- ○ draw

3 **Where was Pam in picture 3?**

- ○ park
- ○ school
- ○ house

4 **What did Pam's mother do?**

- ○ She went skating.
- ○ She helped Pam.
- ○ She read a book.

5 **In picture 2, how can you tell that Pam was sad?**

____

____

Fresh Reads   Unit R Week 1 OL

Name ______________________________

Read the selection. Then answer the questions that follow.

Sam's Books

I see the books. One is green. One is yellow. Two are blue. I like the little green one. I go for the green one. I have my little green book with me.

Mom comes to me. We are on a mat. She looks at the green one with me.

Turn the page.

1 **Where is Sam?**

- ◯ in a car
- ◯ on a mat
- ◯ in a box

2 **What does Sam like to do?**

- ◯ look at a book
- ◯ sleep
- ◯ brush his teeth

3 **Who is with Sam?**

- ◯ a baby
- ◯ Dad
- ◯ Mom

4 **Which book does Sam like?**

____

____

____

5 **How does Mom feel?**

____

____

____

Name ___________________________

Look at the pictures. Then answer the questions that follow.

What Fun!

Turn the page.

1 **Where was the girl in the *first* picture?**

- ◯ in a pool
- ◯ at the beach
- ◯ in a park

2 **What did the girl like to do?**

- ◯ play
- ◯ read
- ◯ sleep

3 **When did the story take place?**

- ◯ in the fall
- ◯ in the summer
- ◯ in the winter

4 **Where was the girl in the *last* picture?**

____

____

____

____

____

____

____

____

Name ________________

Look at the pictures. Then answer the questions that follow.

Mat's Day

1

2

3

4

Turn the page.

Answer the questions below.

1 **Where was Mat in the *first* picture?**

- ○ on a bus
- ○ in the yard
- ○ in the kitchen

2 **Where was Mat in the *second* picture?**

- ○ on a bus
- ○ at school
- ○ in a park

3 **What did Mat like to do in the park?**

- ○ ride his bike
- ○ run on a path
- ○ sit on a bench

4 **Where was Mat in the *last* picture?**

- ○ in his classroom
- ○ in his bedroom
- ○ in a car

5 **Where was Mat in the *first* and *last* pictures?**

____

- -

____

- -

____

Fresh Reads   Unit R Week 2 OL

Read the selection. Then answer the questions that follow.

Where Are You, Pat?

Mom said, "Where are you, Pat?"

"On a plane with Sam," said Pat.

She said, "Where are you, Pat?"

"In a car with Pam," said Pat.

She said, "Where are you, Pat?"

"On a bus with Nan," said Pat.

She said, "Come out of the tub, Pat. I can see you. Come

here with me. We have to go."

Turn the page.

Answer the questions below.

1 **Where did Pat say she was *first*?**

- ○ on a bus
- ○ in a bed
- ○ on a plane

2 **Where did Pat say she was *second*?**

- ○ in a car
- ○ on a boat
- ○ in bed

3 **How did Pat feel in this story?**

- ○ She was mad.
- ○ She was happy.
- ○ She was sleepy.

4 **Where did Pat say she was *last*?**

____

- -

____

____

- -

____

5 **Where was Pat all the time?**

____

- -

____

____

- -

____

Fresh Reads   Unit R Week 2 A

Name ______________________________

Look at the pictures. Then answer the questions that follow.

Getting Ready

1

2

3

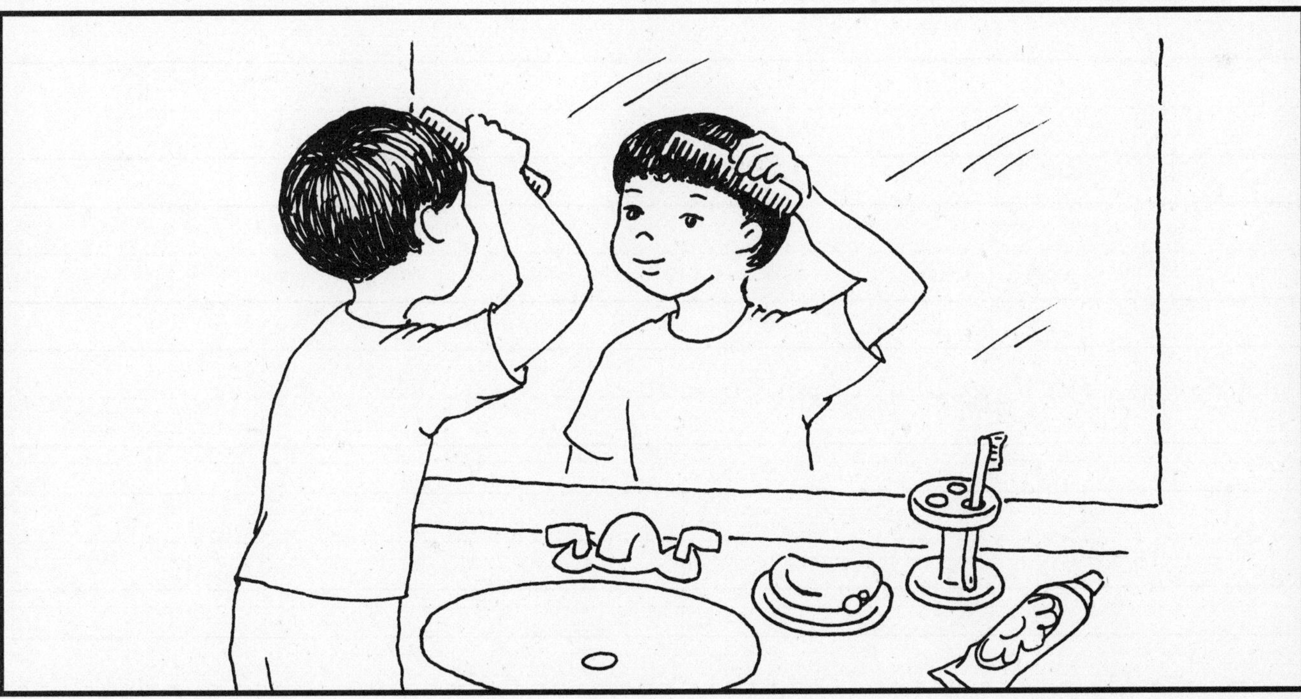

Turn the page.

Answer the questions below.

1 **What was the *first* thing the boy used?**

○ a comb

○ a wash cloth

○ a toothbrush

2 **What did the boy use *next*?**

○ a toothbrush

○ a bar of soap

○ a comb

3 **Where was the boy?**

○ He was in his bedroom.

○ He was in the bathroom.

○ He was in the kitchen.

4 **What did the boy do *last*?**

____

____

____

____

____

____

____

____

Fresh Reads   Unit R Week 3 SI

Name ____

Look at the pictures. Then answer the questions that follow.

Dinner Time

1

2

3

4

Turn the page.

Answer the questions below.

1 **What did the mom do at the *beginning* of the story?**

   ○ Mom ate a meal.

   ○ Mom cut a carrot.

   ○ Mom set the table.

2 **What did the mom do *next*?**

   ○ Mom read a book.

   ○ Mom cleaned the table.

   ○ Mom cooked a meal.

3 **What did the boy do in the *third* picture?**

   ○ The boy set the table.

   ○ The boy ate a meal.

   ○ The boy cooked a meal.

4 **Where did this story take place?**

   ○ at a store

   ○ at home

   ○ at school

5 **What did the family do *last*?**

____

- -

____

- -

____

Name _______________________________

Read the selection. Then answer the questions that follow.

Leaves

Dad, Biff, and Tim go in the car. They go to look at leaves.

Tim said, "I see green ones. I see yellow ones."

Tim can see yellow leaves on the ground. "Look! Here are big ones. We can fit three in a bag."

At home Tim pins up yellow ones. Tim said, "Come see! We have big yellow ones."

They come to see. Biff looks. He said, "I like big yellow ones."

They said, "We like that."

Turn the page.

Answer the questions below.

1 **What happened at the *beginning* of the story?**

○ Tim was in bed.

○ The family was in a car.

○ Dad got leaves.

2 **What happened in the *middle* of the story?**

○ Tim saw leaves on the ground.

○ Dad got in the car.

○ Biff came to see the leaves.

3 **What did Tim take home?**

○ yellow leaves

○ red leaves

○ green leaves

4 **What happened *last* in the story?**

____

- -

____

____

- -

____

5 **Where was Tim at the *end* of the story?**

____

- -

____

____

- -

____

 Fresh Reads   Unit R Week 3 A

Name ___________________________________

Look at the pictures. Then answer the questions that follow.

Play Date

Turn the page.

Fresh Reads   Unit R Week 4 SI

1 **What did the boy and the frog do at the *beginning* of the story?**

- ○ They rode trikes.
- ○ They played with cars.
- ○ They jumped in a pond.

2 **What told you this story was make-believe?**

- ○ The frog has on clothes.
- ○ The boy has on clothes.
- ○ The boy rode a trike.

3 **What could *not* really happen?**

- ○ A frog can not jump.
- ○ A boy can not play.
- ○ A frog can not ride a trike.

4 **What could really happen in this story?**

____

- -

____

- -

____

- -

____

- -

____

- -

____

Name _______________________________

Look at the pictures. Then answer the questions that follow.

What a Night!

1

2

3

4

Turn the page.

1 **What happened at the *beginning* of the story?**

○ The girl read a book.

○ The girl drove a car.

○ The girl flew on a bed.

2 **What can really happen?**

○ A girl can be on a cloud.

○ A girl can sleep in a bed.

○ A girl can fly a car.

3 **What *can not* be real?**

○ a book with a face

○ a bed in a room

○ a girl in a bed

4 **Where can a bed really be?**

○ flying in the air

○ resting on a cloud

○ sitting in a room

5 **How can you tell this story is make-believe?**

____

____

____

____

____

____

Name _______________________________

Read the selection. Then answer the questions that follow.

The Frog and the Cat

"What can we do?" said the yellow frog.

"We can go to see the blue dog," said the green cat.

"Not me," said the yellow frog.

"Can we look at the big books?" said the green cat.

"We can!" said the yellow frog.

They look at four books. They like the two blue ones.

They hop on the bed. They have fun.

Turn the page.

1 **Only a make-believe frog can**

○ be green.

○ talk with a cat.

○ sit in water.

2 **What *can not* really happen?**

○ A frog hops high.

○ A cat sees a frog.

○ A frog likes blue books.

3 **What happens at the *end* of the story?**

○ The frog and the cat hop on the bed.

○ The frog plays with the dog.

○ The frog asks the cat questions.

4 **What can really happen?**

____

____

____

____

5 **How can you tell this is make-believe?**

____

____

____

____

Name _______________________________

Look at the pictures. Then answer the questions that follow.

Jill Has Fun

1

2

3

Turn the page.

Answer the questions below.

1 **What happened at the *beginning* of the story?**

- ◯ Jill jumped rope.
- ◯ Jill went down a slide.
- ◯ Jill rested in a hammock.

2 **What happened in the *middle* of the story?**

- ◯ Jill played on a swing.
- ◯ Jill played with a dog.
- ◯ Jill played with a ball.

3 **What could *not* really happen?**

- ◯ Jill is bigger than her house.
- ◯ Jill climbs a ladder.
- ◯ Jill plays with a ball.

4 **What happened at the *end* of the story?**

____

____

____

____

____

____

____

Name _______________________________

Look at the pictures. Then answer the questions that follow.

Rain and Sun

1

2

3

4

Turn the page.

Fresh Reads   Unit R Week 5 OL

Answer the questions below.

1 How does the story *begin*?

- ○ The boys go out.
- ○ The boys talk.
- ○ The boys play.

2 In the *middle* of the story, the boys want to

- ○ play with a ball.
- ○ go home.
- ○ look at frogs.

3 What would make this story make-believe?

- ○ The boys are friends.
- ○ The ball gets wet.
- ○ The sun talks.

4 In the *middle* of the story, why can't the boys play?

- ○ It is raining.
- ○ The sun is out.
- ○ They do not have a ball.

5 How does the story *end*?

Fresh Reads   Unit R Week 5 OL

Name _______________________________________

Read the selection. Then answer the questions that follow.

The New School

Dan is at a new school. He wants to have a pal. He likes to jog with a pal. He likes to hop with a pal.

One day, Sam comes to the school. He has a red cap. He is new like Dan. Dan can see Sam on the yellow bus. He can sit with Sam. Dan likes Sam.

Dan and Sam are pals. They are at the top of a hill. They hit a ball with a bat. They let the ball hit a can.

Turn the page.

Fresh Reads   Unit R Week 5 A

1 **What happens at the *beginning* of the story?**

- ○ Dan plays a little ball.
- ○ Dan is at a new school.
- ○ Dan is on a big hill.

2 **What does Dan like to do with a pal?**

- ○ jog
- ○ read
- ○ win

3 **How do you know this story could really happen?**

- ○ Dan can fly home.
- ○ Dan is a tan cat.
- ○ Dan is at a school.

4 **What does Dan do *after* he sees Sam?**

____

____

____

5 **What happens at the *end* of the story?**

____

____

____

Name ______________________________

Look at the picture. Then answer the questions that follow.

The Picnic

Turn the page.

Fresh Reads   Unit R Week 6 SI

Answer the questions below.

1 **What *can not* really happen?**

- ⭕ Bears eat some food.
- ⭕ Bears read a paper.
- ⭕ Bears have a family.

2 **Only a make-believe bear can**

- ⭕ have paws.
- ⭕ see a tree.
- ⭕ wear a hat.

3 **Where were the bears?**

- ⭕ in a school
- ⭕ in a park
- ⭕ in a house

4 **How can you tell this story is make-believe?**

____

- -

____

- -

____

- -

____

- -

____

Name ______________________________

Look at the pictures. Then answer the questions that follow.

School Days

Turn the page.

Answer the questions below.

1 **Where *are* the animals?**

- ○ in school
- ○ on a bus
- ○ at home

2 **What can really happen?**

- ○ A dog goes to school.
- ○ A cat takes a nap.
- ○ A cow jumps a rope.

3 **What *can not* really happen?**

- ○ A school has toys.
- ○ A teacher reads books.
- ○ A cat goes to school.

4 **A real school does *not* have**

- ○ books.
- ○ balls.
- ○ cows.

5 **How can you tell this story is make-believe?**

____

- -

____

____

- -

____

____

- -

____

Name ______________________________

Read the selection. Then answer the questions that follow.

The Cat and the Pig

Jen is a little cat. Sid is a big pig. Jen and Sid went to a red mat.

The mat said, "Nap on me!"

Sid sat on the red mat. He said, "You are little. I can not nap on you."

Jen sat on the mat. Jen said, "Look! I fit on the red mat. I can nap on it."

Sid flew to a blue mat. It said, "Nap on me!"

Sid sat on the blue mat. He said, "I fit on the blue mat! I can nap on it."

Turn the page.

Fresh Reads   Unit R Week 6 A

1 **What *can not* really happen?**

- ◯ A mat can be blue.
- ◯ A pig can look.
- ◯ A cat can talk.

2 **Where does Sid nap?**

- ◯ on a red mat
- ◯ on a blue mat
- ◯ on a green mat

3 **What can a real pig do?**

- ◯ fly
- ◯ talk
- ◯ nap

4 **What in this story can really happen?**

____

____

____

5 **How can you tell this story is make-believe?**

____

____

____

Name ________________________

Look at the pictures. Then answer the questions that follow.

Jason Learns to Ride

Turn the page.

1 **What did Jason do *first*?**

○ He rode his bike.

○ He put on his helmet.

○ He got help from Mom.

2 **How did Jason feel *before* he rode his bike?**

○ happy

○ sleepy

○ scared

3 **How did Jason feel *after* he rode his bike?**

○ happy

○ sad

○ angry

4 **How does Jason feel about riding a bike?**

____

- -

____

- -

____

- -

____

- -

____

Name ___________________________

Look at the pictures. Then answer the questions that follow.

The Playful Girl

1

2

3

Turn the page.

Answer the questions below.

1 **What did the girl do *first?***

- ○ She watched the rain.
- ○ She played ball.
- ○ She rode her bike.

2 **What does the girl like to do?**

- ○ She likes to play.
- ○ She likes to sit.
- ○ She likes to read.

3 **How does the girl feel when she plays?**

- ○ sad
- ○ happy
- ○ tired

4 **How does the girl feel when it rains?**

- ○ happy
- ○ sleepy
- ○ sad

5 **What does the girl like doing outside?**

Name ______________________________

Read the selection. Then answer the questions that follow.

Dan's Cat

Dan has a little cat. The cat is Rags. Dad is mad at Rags.
Rags gets in Dad's bag. Dad can see Dan and Rags. Dan and
Rags have fun in the hot sun. Then, Rags naps on Dan's lap.
Dan pats Rags on the back. Rags is happy. Dan likes to have
Rags as a pal.

Turn the page.

Answer the questions below.

1 **Why is Dad mad?**

- ○ Rags hurt Dad.
- ○ Rags gets in Dad's bag.
- ○ Rags is lost.

2 **How does Dan feel about Rags?**

- ○ mad
- ○ sad
- ○ glad

3 **What does Rags do just *after* Rags and Dan have fun in the sun?**

- ○ Rags takes a nap.
- ○ Rags gets in Dad's bag.
- ○ Rags jumps in a box.

4 **What does Dan do for Rags?**

____

- -

____

- -

____

5 **How does Rags feel about Dan?**

____

- -

____

- -

____

Fresh Reads   Unit 1 Week 1 A

Name _______________________________

Look at the pictures. Then answer the questions that follow.

The Lion and the Monkey

1

2

3

4

Turn the page.

1 **What happened *first* in the story?**

- ◯ The lion grew hungry.
- ◯ The lion met the monkey.
- ◯ The lion ate some food.

2 **The monkey was**

- ◯ kind to the lion.
- ◯ mean to the lion.
- ◯ afraid of the lion.

3 **What happened right *after* the lion met the monkey?**

- ◯ The monkey grew hungry.
- ◯ The monkey ran away from him.
- ◯ The monkey told him to come.

4 **What happened *last* in the story?**

____

____

____

____

____

____

____

Name ___________________________

Look at the pictures. Then answer the questions that follow.

Fun at the Beach

1

2

3

4

Turn the page.

Answer the questions below.

1 **How does the mouse feel?**

- ○ happy
- ○ sad
- ○ mad

2 **What happens *first* in the story?**

- ○ The mouse digs in the sand.
- ○ The frog jumps on the beach.
- ○ The pig reads a book.

3 **What happens in the *middle* of this story?**

- ○ The frog jumps on the beach.
- ○ The mouse digs in the sand.
- ○ The fox has a picnic lunch.

4 **What happens right *before* the fox has lunch?**

- ○ The pig reads.
- ○ The frog jumps.
- ○ The mouse digs.

5 **What happens *last* in the story?**

____

____

Fresh Reads Unit 1 Week 2 OL

Name _______________________________

Read the selection. Then answer the questions that follow.

Max on a Trip

Dear Ken,

I was on a trip with my cat, Sam. I had on my big hat. I had a pack on my back.

Sam had on a cap. It was tan.

We saw Tim. Tim was a big green pig.

Tim said, "Come and play tag with me!" We did. We had fun in the sun. Sam and I ran up a hill. Tim said, "I will tag you, Sam." He did.

Next we had a fig and a nap.

In the end, Sam and I went home.

From,

Max

Turn the page.

Fresh Reads   Unit 1 Week 2 A

Answer the questions below.

1 **What did Max do at the *beginning* of the trip?**

○ got on a hat

○ had a nap

○ played tag

2 **Max is**

○ mean.

○ silly.

○ sad.

3 **What happened *after* Sam and Max met Tim?**

○ They played tag.

○ They saw a pig.

○ They went on a trip.

4 **What did Max do right *after* he had a fig?**

____

____

____

5 **What did Max do *after* his trip?**

____

____

____

Fresh Reads   Unit 1 Week 2 A

Name _______________________________

Look at the pictures. Then answer the questions that follow.

Ling Plays Ball

Turn the page.

Answer the questions below.

1 **Ling likes to**

○ play t-ball.

○ take walks.

○ cook.

2 **Where does this story take place?**

○ at Ling's home

○ at a park

○ at a store

3 **How did Ling feel when she hit the ball?**

○ sad

○ angry

○ happy

4 **How can you tell this story could really happen?**

____

____

____

____

____

____

Name ______________________________

Look at the picture. Then answer the questions that follow.

On a Trip

Turn the page.

Answer the questions below.

1 The boy and the dog are

- ○ friendly.
- ○ mean.
- ○ mad.

2 How can you tell this story is make-believe?

- ○ The boy has a pet dog.
- ○ The boy and the dog are in space.
- ○ There are stars.

3 How does the boy feel?

- ○ happy
- ○ angry
- ○ scared

4 Where does this story happen?

- ○ in a park
- ○ at a school
- ○ in space

5 How does Zam feel when he sees the boy and dog?

____

____

____

____

Name _______________________________

Read the selection. Then answer the questions that follow.

Fox's Box

Fox got in the big box at the pond. It was fun. But the box fell in. It did not stop. Fox got mad. He did not like to get wet. He did not like the box. It was not fun. He had to get back to land.

"Help!" Fox said.

"Come here!" said Rob.

"Where are you?" said Fox.

"I am here. Hop in!" said Rob. "You can do it! Come with me!"

Fox did it, and he got back.

Turn the page.

1 **Where was Fox?**

- ◯ on a hill
- ◯ at a pond
- ◯ at his house

2 **How did Fox feel when the box fell in the pond?**

- ◯ silly
- ◯ happy
- ◯ mad

3 **Rob liked to**

- ◯ help.
- ◯ run.
- ◯ sit.

4 **How did Fox feel at the *end* of the story?**

____

- -

____

- -

____

5 **How did you know this story was make-believe?**

____

- -

____

____

- -

____

- -

Name ____

Look at the pictures. Then answer the questions that follow.

The Family

Turn the page.

1 **What is the story *mostly* about?**

- ○ a new baby
- ○ food
- ○ grandparents

2 **What would be another good title for this story?**

- ○ A Big House
- ○ Baby Comes Home
- ○ Time for Bed

3 **What does the family do at the *end* of the story?**

- ○ play with the baby
- ○ play with toys
- ○ play outside

4 **Why do you think the family looks tired at breakfast?**

____

- -

____

- -

____

- -

____

Name ___________________

Look at the pictures. Then answer the questions that follow.

The Builders

Turn the page.

Fresh Reads   Unit 1 Week 4 OL

Answer the questions below.

1 **Who do these pictures tell about?**

- ○ a girl
- ○ a family
- ○ a girl and a boy

2 **What is this story *mostly* about?**

- ○ A boy and a girl build with blocks.
- ○ A girl helps.
- ○ A boy makes something.

3 **The boy and girl**

- ○ work together.
- ○ play ball.
- ○ read to each other.

4 **What is another good title for this story?**

- ○ A Block
- ○ A Tall Building
- ○ A Little Boy

5 **What happens at the *end* of the story?**

____

- -

____

____

- -

____

Name ___________________________________

Read the selection. Then answer the questions that follow.

Bob's Job

Bob gets back from town. He has to get dinner for his animals. He likes to do it. He takes seeds to them.

"Eat this up! It will help you get big!"

The animals like to eat. Lots of little birds come to eat. Bob likes to look. He sees five yellow ones. He sees two blue ones. Bob likes his job. It is fun.

Turn the page.

Fresh Reads   Unit 1 Week 4 A

Answer the questions below.

1 **What was this story *mostly* about?**

- ◯ playing in the yard
- ◯ getting big and strong
- ◯ feeding animals and watching birds

2 **What is another good title for this story?**

- ◯ Yellow Birds
- ◯ Bob and the Animals
- ◯ Birds Fly Away

3 **Why did lots of little birds come?**

- ◯ They came to eat.
- ◯ They wanted to play.
- ◯ They were hot.

4 **Why did Bob have seeds?**

____

- -

____

- -

____

5 **What happened at the *end* of the story?**

____

- -

____

- -

____

Fresh Reads   Unit 1 Week 4 A

Name _______________________________

Look at the pictures. Then answer the questions that follow.

Camping

Turn the page.

Fresh Reads   Unit 1 Week 5 SI

Answer the questions below.

1 **Where did this story take place?**

- ○ in a city
- ○ in a house
- ○ in a forest

2 **What was this story *mostly* about?**

- ○ camping
- ○ gardening
- ○ jumping

3 **What was the *middle* picture all about?**

- ○ riding to the woods
- ○ setting up the camp
- ○ having fun after dark

4 **When did the story *end*?**

Fresh Reads   Unit 1 Week 5 SI

Name ___________________________

Look at the picture. Then answer the questions that follow.

Jack and the Beanstalk

Turn the page.

1 **What is this story *all* about?**

   ○ when Jack climbs a beanstalk

   ○ what Jack feeds a goose

   ○ how Jack builds a castle

2 **The giant is**

   ○ a young boy.

   ○ a big man.

   ○ an old woman.

3 **What does the giant have in his hand?**

   ○ an egg

   ○ a goose

   ○ a beanstalk

4 **How does Jack feel when he sees the giant?**

   ○ happy

   ○ angry

   ○ scared

5 **What tells you that the story happens in the sky?**

____

____

____

Name _______________________________

Read the selection. Then answer the questions that follow.

Kim's Dinner

Kim and her pals eat dinner on the grass. They see a cat, a pig, and a fox.

Kim said, "Can you hum a song, Cat?"

"Yes!" said Cat. And he did.

"Can you hop on one leg, Pig?" said Kim.

"Yes!" said Pig. And he did.

"Can you do tricks, Fox?" Kim said.

"Yes!" said Fox. And he did.

They had fun.

Turn the page.

Fresh Reads   Unit 1 Week 5 A

Answer the questions below.

1 **Who can hum a song?**

- ◯ Kim
- ◯ Cat
- ◯ Fox

2 **Where did Kim have dinner?**

- ◯ on the grass
- ◯ at school
- ◯ in the park

3 **What was this story *mostly* about?**

- ◯ Kim and her pals read a story.
- ◯ Kim and her pals had a race.
- ◯ Kim and her pals had fun.

4 **What did Pig do?**

____

____

____

5 **What did Fox do?**

____

____

____

Fresh Reads   Unit 1 Week 5 A

Name ________________________

Look at the pictures. Then answer the questions that follow.

Dad and Anna Go Shopping

1

2

3

4

Turn the page.

Answer the questions below.

1 **What did Anna want in picture 1?**

◯ to eat

◯ to sleep

◯ to play

2 **Why did Dad and Anna go shopping?**

◯ They needed food.

◯ They had dropped their eggs.

◯ They were bored.

3 **Why did Dad and Anna clean the floor?**

◯ They went shopping.

◯ Dad spilled milk.

◯ Anna dropped an egg.

4 **Why did Anna drop an egg?**

____

- -

____

____

- -

____

____

- -

____

____

- -

____

Name ______________________________

Look at the pictures. Then answer the questions that follow.

In the Garden

Turn the page.

Answer the questions below.

1 **What grew in the dirt?**

- ⭘ the sun
- ⭘ some water
- ⭘ a plant

2 **Why did the girl and her mom dig a hole?**

- ⭘ They were planting a bush.
- ⭘ They were making mud pies.
- ⭘ They were hiding a box.

3 **Why did the girl water the plant?**

- ⭘ to make it go away
- ⭘ to help it grow
- ⭘ to clean it

4 **Why did the girl and her mom wear gloves?**

- ⭘ to keep their hands safe
- ⭘ to stay warm
- ⭘ to look nice

5 **Why was the girl happy at the *end* of the story?**

____

- -

____

____

- -

____

____

- -

____

Name _______________________________

Read the selection. Then answer the questions that follow.

Ron

Ron is sick. He will not go to class. He is at home with Dad. He will not go to bed for a nap. He can look at an animal book for fun. It has a hippo, an elephant, and a zebra. Next Ron plays with his cat. But Ron must rest. Then Ron will get well.

Turn the page.

Answer the questions below.

1 Why was Ron at home?

- ◯ It was raining.
- ◯ He was sick.
- ◯ It was summer.

2 Why did Ron read a book?

- ◯ He liked zoos.
- ◯ He had homework.
- ◯ He was not tired.

3 Who did Ron play with?

- ◯ his cat
- ◯ his dad
- ◯ his mom

4 Why did Ron have to rest?

____

____

____

5 When will Ron feel better?

____

____

____

Name ______________________________

Look at the pictures. Then answer the questions that follow.

Mr. Cat and Miss Bunny

Turn the page.

1 **What happened *first* in the story?**

- ○ Bunny ate cookies with Cat.
- ○ Bunny came to Cat's house.
- ○ Bunny went home for a nap.

2 **What happened *second* in the story?**

- ○ Cat waved at Bunny.
- ○ Cat poured milk.
- ○ Cat opened the door.

3 **What happened *last* in the story?**

- ○ Cat and Bunny had a snack.
- ○ Cat and Bunny played a game.
- ○ Cat and Bunny said hello.

4 **Why did Bunny come to Cat's house?**

Name _______________________________

Read the selection. Then answer the questions that follow.

Fox Has Fun

Fox likes to jog. She jogs to town. Then she jogs to the
park. As she jogs, she sees bugs. She sees ducks, too. Next,
she sees the sun. Then Fox jogs home. At home, she sees Dad.
She tells him what she saw. She tells him she had lots of fun.
She tells Dad to jog with her. Dad will!

Turn the page.

Answer the questions below.

1 **Why did Fox jog to town?**

   ○ to have fun

   ○ to see Dad

   ○ to get home

2 **Where did Fox jog *first*?**

   ○ to the park

   ○ to her house

   ○ to the town

3 **What did Fox see *first*?**

   ○ the ducks

   ○ the bugs

   ○ the sun

4 **What did Fox see right *after* she saw ducks?**

   ○ the park

   ○ the bugs

   ○ the sun

5 **What did Fox do *last*?**

____

- -

____

____

- -

____

Fresh Reads   Unit 2 Week 1 OL

Name _______________________________

Read the selection. Then answer the questions that follow.

Look, Look, Look!

Fred said, "I want to play ball. Sam and Pam, do you want to play ball with me?"

"Yes!" said Sam and Pam.

Fred asked, "Do you have a ball?"

They did not have a ball. They all went looking for a ball. They went looking at home. They went looking in the park. Then Fred saw his dog Zip. Zip had a ball with him! Then Fred, Sam, Pam, and Zip had fun playing ball in the park.

Turn the page.

Answer the questions below.

1 **What happened *first* in the story?**

- ◯ Fred wanted to find Zip.
- ◯ Fred wanted to play ball.
- ◯ Fred wanted to see the park.

2 **What did Fred ask Sam and Pam *first*?**

- ◯ to get a ball
- ◯ to play with him
- ◯ to look for his dog

3 **Where did they look *after* they looked at home?**

- ◯ in the park
- ◯ at the school
- ◯ on the bed

4 **Why did they go looking at home?**

____

- -

____

- -

____

5 **What happened *last* in the story?**

____

- -

____

____

- -

____

  Fresh Reads Unit 2 Week 1 A

Name ___________________________

Look at the pictures. Then answer the questions that follow.

Jane's Juice

1

2

3

4

Turn the page.

Answer the questions below.

1 Where does Jane drink juice?

   ○ at her home

   ○ at her school

   ○ at a park

2 What happens when Jane drinks her juice?

   ○ She gets thirsty.

   ○ She gives juice to her brother.

   ○ She starts to cool off.

3 Why does Jane spill her juice?

   ○ The boy opened the door.

   ○ The ball bumped Jane's glass.

   ○ The boy bumped into Jane.

4 Why does Jane drink juice?

Fresh Reads   Unit 2 Week 2 SI

Name _______________________________

Read the selection. Then answer the questions that follow.

What Mom Makes

Sam is six! Mom wants to make a little cake for him. She must mix it up. Then she bakes the cake. It is yellow. Sam likes yellow. Sam's pals come to his home. Mom gets the cake for them. They sit and eat it. It is good! Mom could have made a big cake!

Turn the page.

1 **How did Sam feel about his cake?**

- ○ sad
- ○ mad
- ○ happy

2 **Why did Mom make the cake?**

- ○ Sam was six.
- ○ It was her big day.
- ○ She wanted to eat cake.

3 **Why did Sam's pals come to his home?**

- ○ to eat cake
- ○ to see Mom
- ○ to bake a cake

4 **Why did Mom make a yellow cake?**

- ○ Mom likes yellow.
- ○ Sam likes yellow.
- ○ Sam's pals like yellow.

5 **Why could Mom have made a big cake?**

Name ___________________________________

Read the selection. Then answer the questions that follow.

Nate Gets to Play

Nate plays in the park with his mom. He runs and he
jumps. He plays in the sand. He makes animals with the sand.
Then the rain falls, and Nate must go home. At home Nate
puts on dry socks. Then he takes a nap. Nate wakes up and
sees that the sun is back. Nate smiles. He gets up and walks
back to the park with his mom. He is glad that the sun shines.

Turn the page.

1 **Why did Nate go to the park?**

○ to have fun

○ to see the rain

○ to take a nap

2 **Why did Nate go home?**

○ It was too hot.

○ He was sick.

○ The rain fell.

3 **What did Nate do *after* he put on dry socks?**

○ He played in the sand.

○ He took a nap.

○ He went home.

4 **Why did Nate put on dry socks?**

5 **Why did Nate smile at the *end* of the story?**

Name _______________________________

Look at the pictures. Then answer the questions that follow.

Bike Safety

Fresh Reads   Unit 2 Week 3 SI

Answer the questions below.

1 **The author wanted you to**

- ○ know about the girl's family.
- ○ learn how to ride a bike.
- ○ stay safe while riding a bike.

2 **Why did the author write this?**

- ○ to make you laugh
- ○ to teach you something
- ○ to tell a make-believe story

3 **Which sentence tells about the pictures?**

- ○ The girl needs to be careful.
- ○ The girl likes to run.
- ○ The bike is new.

4 **Why do you think the author used two pictures of the girl?**

Name _______________________________

Read the selection. Then answer the questions that follow.

We See Animals

We can see animals in many places. I have a cat at home. A red bird has a nest in my back tree. Animals live at the animal park too. We see the little whales that live there. We see hippos in the pond. At home or at the animal park, we can see many animals.

Turn the page.

Answer the questions below.

1 **The author wants you to**

○ look at many little red birds.

○ see many tall green trees.

○ see that animals live in many places.

2 **Why does the author write about his cat?**

○ It is one animal he sees.

○ It is the pet he likes most.

○ He does not have a dog.

3 **What does the author like *best*?**

○ homes

○ animals

○ parks

4 **The author does *not* try to**

○ tell about hippos.

○ talk about the animal park.

○ make you sad.

5 **What is this story *mostly* about?**

____

- -

____

____

- -

____

____

- -

____

Name _______________________________________

Read the selection. Then answer the questions that follow.

I Like My Neighborhood

I am a big cat. I am glad I live on Pine Drive. My neighborhood has nice people. The man in the yellow house feeds me. The mail people stop to pet me. Miss Smith puts out milk for me. The milk is good. The mice are not too busy to chase me. The birds sing to me all the time. My neighborhood is the best place!

Turn the page.

1 **Why did the author write this story?**

- ○ to make you smile
- ○ to make you cry
- ○ to make you mad

2 **Who told this story?**

- ○ the birds
- ○ the cat
- ○ the mice

3 **Why did the author write about milk?**

- ○ The author does not like milk.
- ○ The cat likes milk.
- ○ There is no water.

4 **What was this story *mostly* about?**

____

- -

____

- -

____

5 **How did the author make this story funny?**

____

- -

____

- -

____

Name ________________________________

Look at the pictures. Then answer the questions that follow.

Jack Needs a Snack

1

2

3

4

Turn the page.

Answer the questions below.

1 **Why did Jack make a sandwich?**

○ His dad told him to make one.

○ He was hungry.

○ He wanted to feed the cat.

2 **What happened *first* in the story?**

○ Jack poured some milk.

○ Jack ate a sandwich.

○ Jack read a book.

3 **What happened *second* in the story?**

○ Jack made a sandwich.

○ Jack left the kitchen.

○ Jack drank some milk.

4 **What was the *last* thing that happened in the story?**

Name ____

Read the selection. Then answer the questions that follow.

Nice People

Kim came into my class late in the fall. No one said much to her. Then at lunch Jan sat with Kim. Kim was glad. Jan gave grapes to Kim. Kim gave cake to Jan. Then they were pals.

When Jeff came to class, Kim was nice to him. She said, "We can all sit together at lunch."

Turn the page.

Answer the questions below.

1 **Why did Jan give grapes to Kim?**

○ She wanted to be nice to Kim.

○ She had too many grapes.

○ She wanted to eat cake.

2 **What happened *first*?**

○ Jeff came to class.

○ Jan spoke to Kim.

○ Kim came to class.

3 **What happened *after* the girls had lunch?**

○ Kim sat down with Jan.

○ They got to be good friends.

○ Jan went to a new school.

4 **What happened *last*?**

○ Kim sat with Jan.

○ Kim spoke to Jeff.

○ Jeff came to class.

5 **What happened *after* Jan gave Kim grapes?**

____

____

____

Name ____

Read the selection. Then answer the questions that follow.

My Cake for Bill

My name is Jill. My twin is Bill. We are now six! I want to make a cake for Bill. I mix it up. I put it into a pan. Then Mom and I bake the cake. We put yellow frosting on it. I put six candles on the cake. Mom lit them. We sing to Bill. He claps his hands. Then he puffs and puffs but he can not make the candles go out. They are trick candles. What fun!

Turn the page.

1 The *first* thing Jill did to the cake was

○ bake it.

○ mix it.

○ put it in a pan.

2 *After* Jill put frosting on the cake, she

○ put candles on it.

○ clapped her hands.

○ helped Bill.

3 What did Bill do *last*?

○ clap

○ bake

○ blow

4 Why did Mom and Jill sing to Bill?

____

____

____

5 What could Bill do *next*?

____

____

____

Name ______________________________

Look at the picture. Then answer the questions that follow.

The Silly Race

Turn the page.

Answer the questions below.

1 **Why does Jan Todd have her name on the book?**

- ◯ She ran the race.
- ◯ She wrote the story.
- ◯ She was the mouse.

2 **Why do you think the author wrote *The Silly Race?***

- ◯ to teach you about races
- ◯ to tell you about pets
- ◯ to make you laugh

3 **Why are there make-believe animals in the book?**

- ◯ to make the story funny
- ◯ to tell how to win a race
- ◯ to show how animals live

4 **Why is Mouse smiling?**

Fresh Reads   Unit 2 Week 5 SI

Name _______________________________

Read the selection. Then answer the questions that follow.

My Brave Mom

My mom has a good job. Her job is to put out fires. She puts on a big black hat with a wide brim for her job. She drives a red truck. She helps people in the neighborhood. She is brave. I am glad when she comes home safe. When I grow up, I want to put out fires too.

Turn the page.

1 **Why does the author want to put out fires?**

- ○ He wants to be like his mom.
- ○ He likes to put on black hats.
- ○ He wants to ride in red trucks.

2 **Why did the author write this story?**

- ○ to tell about a red truck
- ○ to tell about his mom
- ○ to tell about his neighborhood

3 **Why does Mom put on a hat?**

- ○ to get help
- ○ to look good
- ○ to be safe

4 **Why did the author tell about Mom's hat?**

- ○ to tell when it will rain
- ○ to tell where she lives
- ○ to tell what she looks like

5 **Why does the author think his mom is brave?**

Name _______________________________

Read the selection. Then answer the questions that follow.

A New Pal

Dear Kip,

I have a new pal. He just came to this neighborhood. He lives down the block from me. His name is Jack. He is fun. He is nice too. Jack likes to play ball. He can hit the ball far. He likes to run races. He can run fast. We play together all the time. We have a good time. I am glad I met him.

Still your good pal,

Rick

Turn the page.

Answer the questions below.

1 **Why is the name of this story "A New Pal"?**

- ○ It is about Jack.
- ○ It is about a race.
- ○ It is about a ball.

2 **The author wants Rick's letter to seem**

- ○ sad.
- ○ real.
- ○ silly.

3 **Which of these tells how Rick feels about Jack?**

- ○ His name is Jack.
- ○ He can run fast.
- ○ I am glad I met him.

4 **Why does Rick like Jack?**

____

____

____

5 **How can you tell Rick and Kip are pals?**

____

____

____

Name _______________________________

Look at the pictures. Then answer the questions that follow.

Seasons

Turn the page.

1 **What is the same in each picture?**

- ○ the lamps
- ○ the weather outside
- ○ the snow

2 **The author wants you to**

- ○ learn how birds fly.
- ○ feel sad when it rains.
- ○ see how the weather changes.

3 **Which things are in all three pictures?**

- ○ the boy, the bed, the lamps
- ○ the bed, the snow, the curtains
- ○ the boy, the rain, the lamps

4 **What is different in all the pictures?**

Name ____

Read the selection. Then answer the questions that follow.

A Family

A family can be big or small. Dan has a family with a mom, dad, and nine children. Ann lives with just her mom. Tom lives with his dad. Ben lives with his mom and his dad. Max has a family that lives together in a big neighborhood. Pete has family in many places. A family can come in many shapes and sizes!

Turn the page.

1 **Who has a big family?**

- ◯ Ann
- ◯ Dan
- ◯ Tom

2 **Who has a small family?**

- ◯ Ann
- ◯ Dan
- ◯ Pete

3 **Why does the author say that a family can be big or small?**

- ◯ to show how families are the same
- ◯ to show how families are different
- ◯ to show different kinds of houses

4 **How is Max's family *not* like Pete's family?**

- ◯ Max's family works hard.
- ◯ Max's family has a son.
- ◯ Max's family lives together.

5 **How are Ann's family and Tom's family the same?**

____

- -

____

- -

____

Name ______________________________

Read the selection. Then answer the questions that follow.

Two Rabbits

Two rabbits left the pet shop to live with a new family.
Honey was a tan rabbit. She could live inside. Flower was a
white rabbit. He lived outside in a cage. Honey wanted to eat
carrots and hay. Flower wanted to eat hay and rabbit food.
Honey and Flower liked to hop around their new homes.
Honey and Flower had little noses. They were nice rabbits.

Turn the page.

1 **The author wrote this story to tell you about**

- ◯ a new family.
- ◯ all animals.
- ◯ two rabbits.

2 **How are Honey and Flower the same?**

- ◯ They are tan.
- ◯ They live with a family.
- ◯ They are white.

3 **How is Honey _not_ like Flower?**

- ◯ Honey lives inside.
- ◯ Honey is big.
- ◯ Honey likes to hop.

4 **What do both rabbits like to eat?**

____

- -

____

- -

____

5 **How do the rabbits _not_ look the same?**

____

- -

____

- -

____

Name _______________________________

Read the selection. Then answer the questions that follow.

Jen Is Six

Jen is six. Mom makes a small cake. Dad has a big red box.

What is in it? Mom grins. Dad smiles. Jen has cake. Then Jen

looks in the box. It is a hat. Jen likes it!

Turn the page.

Fresh Reads   Unit 3 Week 1 SI

1 **What happens *first* in the story?**

- ○ Jen gets a hat.
- ○ Mom makes a cake.
- ○ Dad has a box.

2 **What happens right *after* Dad smiles?**

- ○ Jen has cake.
- ○ Mom grins.
- ○ Dad has a box.

3 **What happens *last* in the story?**

- ○ Dad has a box.
- ○ Mom grins.
- ○ Jen looks in the box.

4 **Why do you think the author wrote this story?**

____

____

____

____

Name ___________________________________

Read the selection. Then answer the questions that follow.

It Is Cold!

Kids like to play in the cold. Big kids skate. They can skate on thick ice. They skate on ponds. Big kids smile.

Small kids ride sleds. They can slide down big, slick hills. Sleds go fast! Small kids grin.

Then kids go back home. It is time to take a hot bath. Then it is time to take a nap!

Turn the page.

Answer the questions below.

1 **What happens *first* in the story?**

- ○ Small kids ride on sleds.
- ○ Big kids skate on ponds.
- ○ The kids take a hot bath.

2 **The author wrote this story to**

- ○ make you feel sad.
- ○ teach you to skate.
- ○ tell you real things.

3 **What happens in the *middle* of the story?**

- ○ The sleds go fast.
- ○ The kids go skate.
- ○ The kids go out to play.

4 **What happens right *after* small kids grin?**

- ○ The kids take a nap.
- ○ The kids skate on ice.
- ○ The kids go home.

5 **What happens *last* in the story?**

____

- -

____

____

- -

____

Fresh Reads   Unit 3 Week 1 OL

Name ____

Read the selection. Then answer the questions that follow.

Twins Get a Home

Jack has a twin. Jill has a twin. Jack looks like Jill. Jill looks like Jack.

Jack and Jill like to sit in the sun. Then Jack and Jill go to a fun home. It has Mom. It has Dad. It has kids. Jack and Jill play with kids. Mom feeds Jack and Jill nice bones.

The twins get big fast. Jack is a black dog. What is Jill?

Turn the page.

- -

Fresh Reads   Unit 3 Week 1 A

Answer the questions below.

1 **What happens *first* in the story?**

- ○ The twins go to a fun home.
- ○ The twins sit in the sun.
- ○ The twins get big fast.

2 **What happens *after* the twins get to the home?**

- ○ They sit in the sun.
- ○ They play with kids.
- ○ They are black dogs.

3 **What happens in the *middle* of the story?**

- ○ Mom feeds the twins.
- ○ Jack looks like Dad.
- ○ Jill looks like Mom.

4 **What happens *last* in the story?**

____

____

5 **Why does the author only tell you the twins are dogs at the *end* of his story?**

____

____

____

Name _________________________________

Read the selection. Then answer the questions that follow.

Dogs and Cats

Kip and Pat are black dogs. Tim and Liz are white cats.

Cats can sit up in trees. Dogs sit under trees.

Tim likes to play with Pat. Liz likes to sit in the sun.

Turn the page.

Answer the questions below.

1 **How are Kip and Pat *alike*?**

- ◯ They can sit in trees.
- ◯ They are black dogs.
- ◯ They play with Tim.

2 **How are Tim and Liz *alike*?**

- ◯ They are white cats.
- ◯ They do not sit in the sun.
- ◯ They can play with Pat.

3 **How is Tim *not* like Liz?**

- ◯ Tim is a black dog.
- ◯ Tim likes to play.
- ◯ Tim sits under trees.

4 **What happens at the *end* of the story?**

____

____

____

____

____

____

Name _______________________________

Read the selection. Then answer the questions that follow.

Robin Sings

Robin did not sing. He hummed. He wanted to sing nice songs like Dove. Robin made a wish. He wished to sing. Then he sat in a tree and sang!

Cat came to the tree. Cat did not sing. Cat went up in the tree. Cat sat by Robin. Cat said Robin had a nice song. Robin was glad to sing at last.

Turn the page.

1 **At the beginning, how is Robin *not* like Dove?**

- ○ Robin is a bird, and Dove is not.
- ○ Dove can sing, and Robin can not.
- ○ Robin can sing, and Dove can not.

2 **How are Robin and Cat *alike*?**

- ○ They can sing a song.
- ○ They sit up in a tree.
- ○ They make a wish.

3 **How are Cat and Dove *alike*?**

- ○ They are animals.
- ○ They sing songs.
- ○ They can hum.

4 **At the end of the story, how are Robin and Dove *alike*?**

- ○ They sit with the cat.
- ○ They sing nice songs.
- ○ They wish to hum.

5 **What happens *last* in the story?**

____

____

____

Name _______________________________

Read the selection. Then answer the questions that follow.

A Nice Spot

Lin and Rose will make a nice spot to sit. Lin rakes up leaves. Work makes Lin hot. He stops to rest. Rose digs up weeds.

Lin takes the leaves. He drops them in a big bag. Rose sets the weeds in a big can.

Lin and Rose sit in the nice spot they made. Lin smiles at Rose. Rose grins at Lin.

Turn the page.

Answer the questions below.

1 **What happens at the *beginning* of the story?**

○ Lin rakes the leaves.

○ Lin smiles at Rose.

○ Lin drops leaves in a bag.

2 **How is Lin *not* like Rose?**

○ He sits in a nice spot.

○ He rakes up leaves.

○ He digs up the weeds.

3 **How are Lin and Rose *alike*?**

○ They rake the leaves.

○ They dig the weeds.

○ They sit in one spot.

4 **How is Rose *not* like Lin?**

____

____

____

____

5 **What do Lin and Rose like to do?**

____

____

____

____

Name _______________________________

Read the selection. Then answer the questions that follow.

Red Foxes

Red foxes are small like cats. Red foxes have nice fur. They can live in many places. Red foxes eat fish and mice. But red foxes are not good pets.

Turn the page.

1 **Which is a statement of opinion?**

- ○ Red foxes have nice fur.
- ○ Red foxes are small like cats.
- ○ Red foxes can eat mice.

2 **Which is a statement of fact?**

- ○ Red foxes eat fish and mice.
- ○ Red foxes are not good pets.
- ○ Red foxes have nice fur.

3 **Which is a statement of opinion?**

- ○ Red foxes live in many places.
- ○ Red foxes are not good pets.
- ○ Red foxes can eat fish.

4 **How are red foxes and cats *alike*?**

Name ___________________________________

Read the selection. Then answer the questions that follow.

Hogs

Hogs are pigs. Hogs and pigs are called swine. Hogs live in big pens called lots. Hogs will sit in the mud when they get hot.

Hogs have thick skin and no fur. Hog skin can be black. Hog skin can be white. It can be red too. Hogs can also have spots.

Hogs look very nice. They smell good. They dig for bugs. Hogs are fun to watch!

Turn the page.

Answer the questions below.

1 Which is a statement of fact from the selection?

- ○ Hogs live in big pens called lots.
- ○ Hogs are fun to watch!
- ○ Hogs look very nice.

2 It is a statement of opinion that

- ○ hogs have no fur.
- ○ hogs sit in the mud.
- ○ hogs smell good.

3 Which is a statement of opinion?

- ○ Hog skin can have spots.
- ○ It is fun to watch hogs.
- ○ Hogs dig for bugs.

4 Which is a statement of fact in the selection?

- ○ Hog skin can be white.
- ○ Hogs look very nice.
- ○ They smell good.

5 What is the *same* about hogs and pigs?

____

____

____

Fresh Reads   Unit 3 Week 3 OL

Name _______________________________

Read the selection. Then answer the questions that follow.

Make a Car

Your family can make fun cars to play with at home. Get a box you can cut up and color. You can also use a plastic milk jug. Make fake wheels from plastic. Make stripes on the sides to make the car look like it can go fast.

You made a nice hot rod! You can race cars with your best friends and family.

Turn the page.

1 **Which is a statement of fact?**

○ You can make fun cars.

○ A car can be made from a box.

○ Hot rods are nice to make.

2 **It is a statement of opinion that**

○ you can make fake wheels.

○ you can use plastic to make cars.

○ box cars make good hot rods.

3 **What is a statement of opinion?**

○ You made a nice hot rod!

○ You can race cars with friends.

○ You can also use a milk jug.

4 **Write a statement of fact based on the selection.**

____

____

____

5 **How are boxes and milk jugs *alike*?**

____

____

____

Name _______________________________

Read the selection. Then answer the questions that follow.

Ann Bakes a Cake

Ann said, "Mom, I want to bake a cake."

Mom said, "I will help you make it."

Ann got a box. It had cake mix in it. Mom got eggs. Mom
and Ann made a nice big cake.

Turn the page.

Fresh Reads   Unit 3 Week 4 SI

1 Why do you think the author wrote "Ann Bakes a Cake"?

- ◯ to tell about a cake
- ◯ to tell about eggs
- ◯ to tell a good story

2 How did the author show you Ann likes to bake?

- ◯ She ate an egg.
- ◯ She made a cake.
- ◯ She got a box.

3 This story was

- ◯ just for some fun.
- ◯ to make you feel sad.
- ◯ all about how to bake.

4 What did Mom do *after* Ann got a box?

Name _______________________________

Read the selection. Then answer the questions that follow.

Fun in the Sun

One fine day, Rob and Tom woke up. It was sunny and nice. Rob said, "Get up quick, Tom." Tom got up fast. They felt happy! They had all day to spend with Dad.

Dad said, "We can ride bikes on the trail by the lake."

Rob grinned. Tom smiled. The small bikes fit in the back of the truck. Then Dad drove Rob and Tom to the big lake. They all had lots of fun in the hot sun.

Turn the page.

1 **Why did the author write this story?**

- ○ to tell about bikes
- ○ to tell about a lake
- ○ to tell about a fun time

2 **What happens in this story?**

- ○ A family rides bikes.
- ○ Dad gets an old bike.
- ○ It rains on them all day.

3 **How do you think the author feels about bikes?**

- ○ He is scared of them.
- ○ He likes to ride them.
- ○ He wishes he had one.

4 **How does the author let you know that Rob and Tom wanted to ride bikes?**

- ○ Rob frowned and Tom cried.
- ○ Rob grinned and Tom smiled.
- ○ Dad drove to the big lake.

5 **How can you tell Rob and Tom were in the same family?**

____

- -

____

- -

____

Name _______________________________

Read the selection. Then answer the questions that follow.

Brave Frog

Frog did not like rain at all. When it rained, Frog did not feel safe. He ran to hide. Then it rained hard and did not stop. Frog hid fast.

Then Frog saw Squirrel in a box. Squirrel needed help to get safe. Rain filled the box up to his neck! Frog had to help fast.

Frog ran in the rain. Frog got Squirrel out of the box. Frog saved Squirrel. Then Frog felt safe in the rain.

Turn the page.

1 **What was this story about?**

- ◯ a squirrel that liked rain
- ◯ a frog that saved a squirrel
- ◯ a girl that needed help

2 **What did the author think about Frog?**

- ◯ Frog was silly.
- ◯ Frog was sad.
- ◯ Frog was brave.

3 **How does the author let you know that Frog has changed?**

- ◯ She says that Frog felt safe.
- ◯ She says that Frog saw Squirrel.
- ◯ She says that Frog hid fast.

4 **Why do you think the author wrote this story?**

____

- -

____

- -

____

5 **What was a lesson for Frog?**

____

- -

____

____

- -

____

Name _______________________________

Read the selection. Then answer the questions that follow.

Take a Ride

Cars and trucks run fast. It is fun to ride in cars. Trains run on tracks. They are quick. Planes fly fast in the sky. It is the most fun to take a ride in a plane!

Turn the page.

Answer the questions below.

1 **Which is a statement of fact?**

   ○ Cars are fun to ride in.

   ○ Planes are the most fun.

   ○ Trains run on tracks.

2 **Which is a statement of opinion?**

   ○ Trucks run fast like cars.

   ○ It is fun to go for car rides.

   ○ Planes fly fast in the sky.

3 **What does the selection tell about *last*?**

   ○ cars

   ○ planes

   ○ trains

4 **What is a statement of opinion about planes in the selection?**

____

- -

____

- -

____

- -

____

- -

____

Name ___________________________________

Read the selection. Then answer the questions that follow.

Ants

Ants make nice homes. They dig deep in the ground to make homes. Ants can make hills for homes too. Ant hills stick up on top of the ground.

Ants live in a big family. They work all the time. Ants walk far to get food. They take it back home to feed others.

Big ants keep ant eggs safe. Baby ants hatch from the eggs. Baby ants are cute.

Ants are fun to watch!

Turn the page.

Answer the questions below.

1 **What is a statement of opinion?**

- ○ Ants live in a family.
- ○ Baby ants are cute.
- ○ Ants keep eggs safe.

2 **What happens *first*?**

- ○ Ants make homes.
- ○ Ants walk for food.
- ○ Ants keep eggs safe.

3 **What is a statement of fact?**

- ○ Ants are fun to watch.
- ○ Ants take food home.
- ○ Ants make nice homes.

4 **What sentence tells a statement of opinion?**

- ○ Big ants keep ant eggs safe.
- ○ Ant hills stick up on top of the ground.
- ○ Ants are fun to watch.

5 **What is a statement of fact about baby ants?**

____

- -

____

- -

____

Fresh Reads   Unit 3 Week 5 OL

Name _______________________________

Read the selection. Then answer the questions that follow.

Green Trees

Some trees get green leaves first. In the fall, the leaves turn red or yellow. They are pretty. Then they drop on the ground. Kids use leaves to make art.

Some trees are green all the time. They are called evergreen trees. Some of them are small. Others grow very big.

Animals like evergreen trees. Birds like to sit in them. Rabbits make homes under them. People like evergreen trees too. Evergreen trees look nice and smell good.

Turn the page.

Answer the questions below.

1 **What happens *last* to some tree leaves?**

- ○ They fall on the ground.
- ○ They turn red or yellow.
- ○ They grow out green.

2 **What tells a statement of opinion?**

- ○ Rabbits can live under trees.
- ○ Trees have green leaves first.
- ○ Some trees smell very good.

3 **What tells a statement of fact?**

- ○ The red leaves are pretty.
- ○ Some trees are green all the time.
- ○ Evergreen trees look nice.

4 **What is a statement of opinion about leaves?**

____

- -

____

- -

____

5 **Write a statement of fact about evergreen trees.**

____

- -

____

____

- -

____

Fresh Reads   Unit 3 Week 5 A

Name _______________________________

Read the selection. Then answer the questions that follow.

Twins

Jane and Mark are twins. Jane was born first. Mark is bigger than Jane. Jane likes to play ball and swim. Mark likes to brush his dog when it is dirty. Mark likes to pet his cat. Jane and Mark like to make forts.

Turn the page.

Fresh Reads   Unit 3 Week 6 SI

Answer the questions below.

1 **How are Mark and Jane the *same*?**

- ◯ They are girls.
- ◯ They make forts.
- ◯ They swim fast.

2 **What do you know about Jane and Mark?**

- ◯ They are not very tall.
- ◯ They like to run races.
- ◯ They are in one family.

3 **What can you tell about Mark?**

- ◯ He likes animals.
- ◯ He has a horse.
- ◯ He can't swim.

4 **How do you know Jane likes to be outside?**

____

____

____

____

Name _______________________________________

Read the selection. Then answer the questions that follow.

A New Place

Jake had to go live in a new place. Mom got a new job. Jake felt sad and just sat on his bed. Then he sat on the rug.

Dad came to see him. Dad sat by Jake and hugged him. Then Jake felt much better. He felt glad for Mom.

Jake went to a new school. He met Tim and Jack in the first week. They all liked to play ball. Jake felt happy at last.

Turn the page.

Answer the questions below.

1 Dad wanted to

- ○ help Jake.
- ○ play with Jake.
- ○ trick Jake.

2 What made Jake feel sad?

- ○ He did not want to go to a new place.
- ○ He had to stay home from school.
- ○ He would miss his Mom and Dad.

3 How was Mom the *same* as Dad?

- ○ She got a new job.
- ○ She was glad to go.
- ○ She hugged Jake.

4 Why was Jake happy at last?

____

____

____

____

5 How do you think Jake met Tim and Jack?

____

____

____

____

Name ________________________________

Read the selection. Then answer the questions that follow.

Games

Ben liked to play all games. He liked hide-and-seek best.
His sister Kris liked to hide. She liked Ben to look for her.

Dad liked to take Ben to ball games. Ben had lots of fun
with Dad at the games.

Mom liked to sing with Ben and Kris. Mom made up a
singing game. Mom sang one part. Then Ben and Kris would
take turns adding the rest. They all liked this fun game!

Turn the page.

Fresh Reads   Unit 3 Week 6 A

Answer the questions below.

1 Why does Ben like all games?

- ⭕ He likes to have fun.
- ⭕ He likes to play with Kris.
- ⭕ He likes to be outside.

2 What makes Kris happy?

- ⭕ to look for Ben
- ⭕ to go to ball games
- ⭕ to hide from Ben

3 How are Dad and Mom the *same*?

- ⭕ They like to go to ball games.
- ⭕ They like to play with the kids.
- ⭕ They like to sing together.

4 Why do you think Ben likes hide-and-seek best?

____

____

____

5 Why do you think Ben likes ball games?

____

____

____

Fresh Reads   Unit 3 Week 6 A

Name ______________________________

Read the selection. Then answer the questions that follow.

Plants

Many people like seeing green plants inside. All plants need lots of sun and nice fresh water. Outside plants get plenty of sunshine and rain. When plants stay inside, people must water them and place them in the sun at times.

Turn the page.

Answer the questions below.

1 **Sunshine makes plants**

○ dark.

○ cold.

○ grow.

2 **What can happen if plants do not get water?**

○ The plants will not live.

○ The plants will become green.

○ The plants will get flowers.

3 **Why do many people have plants in the house?**

○ They want to have food around.

○ They enjoy growing plants inside.

○ They need to have some water.

4 **Why do people have to water inside plants?**

Fresh Reads   Unit 4 Week 1 SI

Name _______________________________

Read the selection. Then answer the questions that follow.

Selling Flowers

Bob came to the park every week to sell picked flowers. He called, "Fresh flowers for sale!"

Lee said, "Sell me ten red roses."

"No red roses for sale," said Bob. "I can sell you red mums or a nice daisy."

"I just like roses," said Lee. "I do not want mums or a daisy."

Bob came back the next week. He had ten red roses to sell to Lee.

Lee said, "I do not want roses. I will take ten red mums and one nice, fresh daisy."

Turn the page.

1 **Why did Bob come to the park?**

○ to sell flowers

○ to visit his family

○ to meet his friends

2 **Why didn't Lee take a daisy?**

○ She likes flowers.

○ She wanted roses.

○ She wanted mums.

3 **Why did Bob bring roses the next week?**

○ Lee asked for them.

○ He liked red flowers best.

○ Lee wanted a daisy.

4 **Why didn't Lee get roses the next week?**

○ She did not like roses.

○ She had gotten roses before.

○ She wanted mums now.

5 **How do you think Bob felt when Lee did not take the roses?**

Name _______________________________________

Read the selection. Then answer the questions that follow.

The Party

Beth was new on our block. She liked us, so she had a party for us at her home. It was lots of fun!

Beth had made a piñata for us to hit. It was shaped like a big red dog. We all got turns hitting it. It did not crack. Then Beth hit it harder. It broke in two! Small bags fell on the ground. We all got little bags. There were fun things to play with inside the bags.

Then Beth let us make a piñata!

Turn the page.

Answer the questions below.

1 **Why did Beth have a party?**

- ○ It was her mother's birthday.
- ○ The family told her to do it.
- ○ She wanted to make friends.

2 **Why did they hit the piñata?**

- ○ to break it open
- ○ to make it bark
- ○ to spin it around

3 **What happened when Beth hit the piñata harder?**

- ○ It came down.
- ○ It did not crack.
- ○ Bags fell out.

4 **Why did they all go to Beth's party?**

____

____

____

____

5 **How did Beth feel after the party ended?**

____

____

____

____

Name _______________________________

Read the selection. Then answer the questions that follow.

Two Birds

Robin did not like to share his tree. His friend
Hummingbird needed a place to make a nest. She said,
"Robin, you can stay in your nest by the trunk. I will make my
nest in the branches. That way, we can stay in the same tree
and be happy."

Turn the page.

Answer the questions below.

1 **What is this story trying to teach?**

- ○ a way to make a nest
- ○ a way to share with others
- ○ a way to be like a bird

2 **What is the big idea in this story?**

- ○ sharing
- ○ robins
- ○ eating

3 **What would be another good name for this story?**

- ○ Bugs in the Trees
- ○ Having Friends
- ○ Working Together

4 **How were the two birds able to live in the same tree together?**

Name _______________________________

Read the selection. Then answer the questions that follow.

Sun and Sea

Sea felt sad. She needed friends. All she could see was the sun and land.

Then Sun called to Sea. "Hi! Can you play with me?"

"But you are up in the sky," said Sea. "How can we play?"

Sun said, "I can shine on land and on sea. I can smile at you."

Sea said, "I can splash and wave at you! We can be friends."

Sea splashed and waved at Sun every day. Sun shone on Sea and smiled when she splashed. They had fun.

Turn the page.

Answer the questions below.

1 **When did Sun and Sea play together?**

- ○ in the dark
- ○ in the day
- ○ at night

2 **What is this story all about?**

- ○ working together to make friends
- ○ saying good-bye
- ○ splashing and talking

3 **Sea and Sun had to find a way to**

- ○ be sad.
- ○ play together.
- ○ go up and down.

4 **What does this story teach you about friends?**

- ○ Friends can help each other.
- ○ Friends need to stay far away.
- ○ Friends can be mean.

5 **How did Sun and Sea become friends?**

____

- -

____

- -

____

- -

____

Name _________________________________

Read the selection. Then answer the questions that follow.

Greg's First Art Show

Greg hopes to be a fine artist. To help him do that, he plans to show his art to people.

Greg thinks he will try new ways to make art. He splashes paint on bags and uses many colors and shapes. He makes shapes such as green boxes and red lines. He adds white stripes and black dots.

At last Greg makes signs for his show. Lots of people come to see his art. They like it very much and tell Greg he will be a great artist one day.

Turn the page.

Fresh Reads   Unit 4 Week 2 A

Answer the questions below.

1 **What is the big idea in this story?**

- ◯ working with others
- ◯ growing as an artist
- ◯ getting paintings on sale

2 **What does Greg learn from painting?**

- ◯ to make people happy
- ◯ to try new things
- ◯ to sell big signs

3 **What would be another good name for this story?**

- ◯ A New Artist
- ◯ Greg's School
- ◯ How to Make Paints

4 **What does this story teach you?**

____

____

____

____

5 **Why does Greg make signs for his show?**

____

____

____

____

Name _______________________________________

Read the selection. Then answer the questions that follow.

Into the Sky!

At one time, people stayed on land or sea. We rode in cars or trains or ships. Then we made planes. Planes let us fly a long way in a short time. Planes can be very big. Lots of us can fit in them. Flying is fun!

Turn the page.

Answer the questions below.

1 **What helps people move into the sky?**

- ◯ ships
- ◯ cars
- ◯ planes

2 **Why is flying a good way to get places?**

- ◯ It is bigger.
- ◯ It is faster.
- ◯ It is longer.

3 **What do big planes do?**

- ◯ fly many people
- ◯ stay on the land
- ◯ float on the sea

4 **What is a statement of opinion about flying?**

____

____

____

____

____

____

Name _______________________________

Read the selection. Then answer the questions that follow.

Pick a Pet

It can be hard to pick a pet. Many animals make good pets.

You may wish for a pet with soft fur. Cats and dogs can play with you inside or outside. Gerbils stay in cages much of the time, like birds. You may wish for birds or fish. Birds have colored feathers. Fish need to be in water.

Every pet needs good food and a safe home. It can be hard to pick the best pet for you!

Turn the page.

Answer the questions below.

1 **What sentence tells a statement of opinion?**

○ Gerbils stay in cages much of the time.

○ It can be hard to pick a pet.

○ Birds have colored feathers.

2 **Why do cats and dogs make good pets?**

○ They need food to eat.

○ They play with people.

○ They need a safe home.

3 **What animal needs to live in water?**

○ cat

○ dog

○ fish

4 **What is a pet that stays in a cage?**

○ a fish

○ a bird

○ a cat

5 **What does every pet need?**

____

____

____

____

  Fresh Reads   Unit 4 Week 3 OL

Name ___________________________

Read the selection. Then answer the questions that follow.

Shells

Shells are hard cases that were part of a sea animal at one time. It is lots of fun to go to sunny, sandy beaches and hunt for shells. You can also get shells in muddy places. After a storm is the best time to hunt for shells. Make sure the place you go lets people pick up shells and take them home. You might pick up clam shells or snail shells. Some people hunt shells for a hobby. All shells look better and feel better when you clean them well.

Turn the page.

Answer the questions below.

1 **What are shells?**

- ○ muddy places
- ○ parts of animals
- ○ sandy beaches

2 **Where can you hunt for shells?**

- ○ on a beach
- ○ at your home
- ○ in hard cases

3 **What shells could you find?**

- ○ whale shells
- ○ fish shells
- ○ clam shells

4 **What should you do before you take shells home?**

____

____

____

____

5 **What is a statement of opinion about shells?**

____

____

____

____

Name ___________________________________

Read the selection. Then answer the questions that follow.

Dog and Cat

Dog did not like Cat near him. But Cat did not leave Dog.

Cat said, "I just like being near dogs."

Dog ran after Cat. Cat went up a tree fast. Cat said, "Why did you chase me?"

Dog said, "I just like to chase cats!"

Turn the page.

1 **Where did Cat run?**

- ○ into the park
- ○ up a tree
- ○ down a street

2 **What did Dog want Cat to do?**

- ○ leave him
- ○ run with him
- ○ chase him

3 **Why did Dog chase Cat?**

- ○ because Cat liked it
- ○ so that Cat would talk
- ○ because Dog liked it

4 **How were Dog and Cat the *same*?**

Fresh Reads   Unit 4 Week 4 SI

Name _______________________________

Read the selection. Then answer the questions that follow.

Big Fish in a Small Lake

A little fish had a nice home in a small lake. He got bigger very fast, until he was the biggest fish in the lake. Still he kept growing bigger. He named himself Big Fish. He needed a bigger home.

Big Fish swam and splashed to the far end of the lake. He swam fast and then jumped up high. He sailed far! When Big Fish landed, he was in the deep blue sea. He swam in the sea and saw many fish bigger than he. Big Fish seemed small in the big sea.

Turn the page.

Answer the questions below.

1 Where did the fish live at the *beginning* of the story?

- ○ in the big sea
- ○ in a small lake
- ○ in a deep pond

2 Why did the fish want to leave?

- ○ He wanted to see more places.
- ○ He liked to fly up in the air.
- ○ He needed a bigger home.

3 How did the fish get to his new place?

- ○ He swam over to it.
- ○ He jumped far.
- ○ He walked there.

4 Where did the fish live at the *end* of the story?

- ○ in the air
- ○ on the land
- ○ in the sea

5 How did the fish feel *after* he moved?

____

____

____

Fresh Reads   Unit 4 Week 4 OL

Name ___________________________

Read the selection. Then answer the questions that follow.

Fun Club

Dear Dad,

Will you take me to the Fun Club? It starts in three days, and we will have lots of fun. We can see many things. We can hear the caterpillar sing. We can see the pig paint its art and then see it fly in the sky. We can feel the goat with red spots. Then we can eat green grapes. They will be yummy! I know we will find things we have never seen. Can we go, Dad? Let me know what you think. Mom will help us plan the trip.

Love,

Jeff

Turn the page.

Answer the questions below.

1 Jeff wants to go to the club with

- ◯ Dad.
- ◯ Mom.
- ◯ friends.

2 What animal paints?

- ◯ a goat
- ◯ a pig
- ◯ a caterpillar

3 What will Jeff eat at the club?

- ◯ candy
- ◯ grapes
- ◯ corn

4 How does Jeff tell about the Fun Club?

____

- -

____

- -

____

5 How are the pig and the caterpillar *alike*?

____

- -

____

____

- -

____

Name _______________________________

Read the selection. Then answer the questions that follow.

Sunny Day

Max played in the sunshine. He liked to play by himself.

Then Carl came over. "May I play with you?" he asked.

Max said, "Yes!"

Carl and Max had fun. Max liked playing with Carl. It was more fun to play with friends than to play by himself.

Turn the page.

Fresh Reads   Unit 4 Week 5 SI

1 **What is the big idea in this story?**

- ○ Summer days are long and hot.
- ○ Playing with others is better.
- ○ Being outside is good for boys.

2 **What does this story show readers?**

- ○ how to play by yourself
- ○ some games for two friends
- ○ a way to have more fun

3 **What would be another good name for this story?**

- ○ Fun with a Friend
- ○ Happy School Days
- ○ The Summer Games

4 **From this story, what can you tell that Carl likes to do?**

Name ______________________________

Read the selection. Then answer the questions that follow.

At the Park

Fred went to the park with his mom. He got on the swing and stayed there. "Fred, share the swing," called his mom. Fred did not share.

Jimmy played ball at the park. His mom called, "Jimmy, share the ball." Jimmy did not share.

"May, share the jump rope," called her mom. May did not share.

Then Kathy came to the park. She said, "We can all make a neat fort if we work together. Come and have fun with me."

The kids came to help. They all made a fort and had fun playing together.

Turn the page.

1 **What is the big idea in this story?**

○ It is good to jump rope.

○ It is hard to make a fort.

○ It is fun to play together.

2 **What is this story trying to teach?**

○ how to make a neat set of swings

○ how to share and play with others

○ how to use snow to put up a fort

3 **What do the kids learn from Kathy?**

○ Sharing is more fun than playing alone.

○ They need more than one jump rope.

○ Fred should take turns on the swing.

4 **What would be a good name for this story?**

○ How to Play Ball

○ Jump Rope Tricks

○ Playing Together

5 **Why do the mothers tell their kids to share things?**

Name ______________________________

Read the selection. Then answer the questions that follow.

Jane's Visit

Mom drove Jane to the animal shelter every week. When Jane got there, she went to see the cats first. She petted all the cats and gave them fresh water. Jane teased the cats with a long string. She smiled at them when they ran to catch it.

Then Jane and Mom went outside to play ball with the dogs. Jane made sure each dog got a pat on the head and a treat from the big jar. Then she took them out for a quick trot on a leash one at a time. When Jane left, she told the pets she would come back soon.

Turn the page.

1 **What is the big idea in this story?**

- ○ playing with your cat
- ○ feeding the pet animals
- ○ helping out at a shelter

2 **What does this story show the reader?**

- ○ You must talk to animals.
- ○ It can be fun to be a helper.
- ○ The dogs are the most fun.

3 **What is another good name for this story?**

- ○ Pick the Right Pet
- ○ Helping Cats and Dogs
- ○ How to Walk a Dog

4 **What has Jane learned from going to the shelter?**

____

____

____

____

5 **How do you know that Jane likes going to the shelter?**

____

____

____

____

Name ___________________________________

Read the selection. Then answer the questions that follow.

Dance Class

Ling did not like dance class. Kids made fun of her.

Every week she asked, "Dad, must I go?"

Dad felt sad. He wished Ling liked class.

Dad said, "Just do your best, and the kids will be nice."

He was right! Ling felt happy.

Turn the page.

Answer the questions below.

1 **How did Ling feel at the *beginning* of the story?**

- ○ happy
- ○ afraid
- ○ sad

2 **Why didn't Ling like her dance class?**

- ○ Other kids picked on her.
- ○ The class was too hard.
- ○ Dad made her go to class.

3 **What made Ling's father sad?**

- ○ He did not want Ling to dance.
- ○ He did not like to drive Ling to class.
- ○ Ling did not like the dance class.

4 **What made Ling happy at the *end* of the story?**

Fresh Reads   Unit 4 Week 6 SI

Name ______________________________

Read the selection. Then answer the questions that follow.

Rose's Plane Trip

Rose and Mom will take a plane trip to see Granny. Granny's home is far away. Rose is a tiny bit scared. She has never gotten on a plane before, and the plane is big!

Rose and Mom wait in long lines. Nice people smile at them. Rose smiles back. Rose starts to feel better. Then it is their turn. Rose and Mom get on the plane. Rose sits by the window and stares at the ground below. Then the plane takes off, and Rose gets snacks. She likes them, and she likes the tray at her seat. Flying is fun!

Turn the page.

- -

Answer the questions below.

1 How did Rose feel at the *beginning* of the story?

- ○ very happy
- ○ a little scared
- ○ hungry and sleepy

2 Why did Rose and Mom go on the plane trip?

- ○ to visit Granny
- ○ to wait in lines
- ○ to eat a snack

3 Rose did not want to fly because

- ○ it was her first time on a plane.
- ○ her mother was there with her.
- ○ the tray at her seat was too big.

4 What made Rose feel better?

- ○ Granny called Rose.
- ○ Rose sat by Mom.
- ○ People smiled at Rose.

5 What made Rose think it was fun to fly?

____

____

____

____

Fresh Reads   Unit 4 Week 6 OL

Name _______________________________

Read the selection. Then answer the questions that follow.

Be Careful!

Jean hurried to get dressed. She wore her new boots with the long laces. She tied the laces in big bows. Jean had to take treats to school. She and Mom had made yummy popcorn balls. When Jean left for school, Mom gave her a big bag of popcorn balls. "Be careful," said Mom. "Do not drop the bag."

Jean went down the back steps. Then she tripped! Her boot lace had come untied. She dropped the bag. Mom quickly picked it up. Jean tightly tied her boot laces. Mom handed Jean the bag again. "Be careful," she said, smiling at Jean.

Turn the page.

1 **Why did Jean need to make popcorn balls?**

○ to take a treat to school

○ to drop on the back steps

○ to eat them with Mom

2 **What made Jean trip?**

○ Her laces came untied.

○ The bag fell at her feet.

○ Mom said to hurry up.

3 **Where did Jean trip?**

○ at her school

○ on the steps

○ at the park

4 **Why did Mom tell Jean to be careful?**

____

- -

____

____

- -

____

5 **Why did Jean tie her boot laces tightly at the *end*?**

____

- -

____

____

- -

____

Name _______________________________________

Read the selection. Then answer the questions that follow.

Hope and the Snake

Hope went to the well for water every day. She carried a bucket to the well and back to her home. She followed the same path every day. One day she met a snake on the path. Hope acted brave. She stopped and stayed very still. She waited. The snake passed, and Hope went on home.

Turn the page.

Answer the questions below.

1 **What is Hope like?**

- ◯ brave
- ◯ silly
- ◯ funny

2 **Where does Hope stand and wait?**

- ◯ in her house
- ◯ on the path
- ◯ in the water

3 **What happens at the *end* of the story?**

- ◯ Hope walks home.
- ◯ Hope sees a snake.
- ◯ Hope stops at the well.

4 **What is the big idea in this story?**

____

____

____

____

____

____

____

____

Name _______________________________

Read the selection. Then answer the questions that follow.

Henry's Train Set

Henry had a train set with bright red train cars. The cars ran on a set of black train tracks. Henry set up the train in his room. He laid the tracks in the shape of an egg. The train tracks went under hills and ran by creeks.

Henry had fun running his train around the tracks. Henry had a little sister named Mary. She asked to play with the train.

"You are too small to know how to run the train," said Henry.

Mary said, "You just do not want to share."

Henry said, "You are right. I am sorry. We can play with the train together."

Turn the page.

Answer the questions below.

1 **What happens at the *beginning* of the story?**

- ◯ Henry sets up his train set in his room.
- ◯ Mary wants to play with the train.
- ◯ Henry asks Mary to play with him.

2 **How do you think Mary feels at the *end* of the story?**

- ◯ too little to play with trains
- ◯ happy that she spoke up
- ◯ afraid of Henry

3 **Where does this story take place?**

- ◯ in the yard
- ◯ at Mary's school
- ◯ in Henry's room

4 **What happens at the *end* of the story?**

- ◯ Henry tells Mary to go away.
- ◯ Henry asks Mary to play.
- ◯ Henry sets up the train tracks.

5 **What is the big idea of this story?**

____

- -

____

Name ______________________________

Read the selection. Then answer the questions that follow.

Big Things

Jed liked big things. He liked big dogs and big cats. He liked big parties and big fun. Jed wished he was bigger!

"When will I get big?" he asked Dad. "I want to be big and tall."

Dad said, "You will get big when you grow more. You will get big at the right time."

Jed was not happy. He wanted to be big now. He went out and hung by his hands for a long time on a tree branch. Maybe that would help him get taller faster. But when he went inside, he was still the same size.

"I think I will just have to wait to get bigger," said Jed.

Turn the page.

1 **Where is Jed at the *beginning* of the story?**

○ in a tree

○ in a school

○ in his house

2 **How does Jed try to get bigger?**

○ He hangs in a tree.

○ He eats more food.

○ He asks Dad for help.

3 **What happens at the *end* of the story?**

○ Jed gets bigger.

○ Jed waits to grow up.

○ Jed grows fast.

4 **How do you think Dad feels about Jed's wish?**

____

____

____

5 **What is the big idea in this story?**

____

____

____

Name _______________________________

Read the selection. Then answer the questions that follow.

Rainy Day

Peg went to the park every day with her dog, Max. She led Max to the park so he could play outside.

One day Peg and Max left for the park. They went down the back steps. Then it started to rain hard. Max did not care that it was raining. Peg got her raincoat, and off they went to the park!

Turn the page.

1 **What is this story all about?**

- ◯ taking good care of your pet
- ◯ going to the park every day
- ◯ wearing raincoats to be dry

2 **How does Peg feel when she walks with Max?**

- ◯ sad
- ◯ angry
- ◯ happy

3 **Why does Peg take Max with her?**

- ◯ Max hates to play in the rain.
- ◯ Max goes everywhere with Peg.
- ◯ Max enjoys going to the park.

4 **Why does Peg get her raincoat?**

Name _________________________________

Read the selection. Then answer the questions that follow.

Dinner for Mom

Mark and Dad will make a chicken dinner for Mom. She will be getting home from a trip. Mark and Dad hope that Mom will feel loved when she gets home. She will not need to make dinner for them.

Mark and Dad clean their hands. Mark and Dad mix up a cake from a box. They bake the cake while they clean the chicken. Then they put salt and pepper on the chicken. They lay the chicken in a long pan. They take the cake out and then bake the chicken. It starts to smell very good just in time. Here is Mom!

Turn the page.

Answer the questions below.

1 **What is this story all about?**

  ○ a smell

  ○ a dinner

  ○ a trip

2 **When is Mom's trip?**

  ○ last week

  ○ that day

  ○ next month

3 **Why do Mark and Dad clean their hands?**

  ○ They are getting ready to eat.

  ○ They are getting ready for bed.

  ○ They are getting ready to cook.

4 **Why do they put salt and pepper on the chicken?**

  ○ to make it taste better

  ○ to make it cleaner

  ○ to make it cook faster

5 **How do you think Mom feels when she gets home?**

Fresh Reads   Unit 5 Week 2 OL

Name ______________________________

Read the selection. Then answer the questions that follow.

Find It!

Sally and Bill went on a fun hunt with some friends. It was a hunt to find things. Each kid had a list of things to find. The first one to bring back all the things on the list would be the winner.

Sally wanted to win. She needed to work fast to get everything on her list. First she went next door and got a feather hat. Then she found a tree and got two red leaves from a branch. She dug a deep hole and got a worm.

Sally got back first with all the things on her list. She was the winner of the fun hunt!

Turn the page.

1 **What was on the lists?**

- ○ things to get as presents
- ○ things that had been lost
- ○ things for them to find

2 **Why did Sally go find a tree?**

- ○ She needed two leaves.
- ○ She needed a branch.
- ○ She needed a worm.

3 **What was this story all about?**

- ○ hunting for birds
- ○ having a contest
- ○ seeing a neighborhood

4 **How did they pick the winner?**

____

____

____

5 **What did Sally have to work the hardest to get?**

____

____

____

Name _______________________________

Read the selection. Then answer the questions that follow.

The Detectives

Greg and Jill are detectives. Greg wanted to find a missing painting. Jill wanted to find a missing ring.

Greg looked for the painting. He saw it in a shop. A man had the painting. He was fixing the frame. Greg smiled. The mystery was solved!

Jill looked for the ring. She looked up and down. She saw the ring in the dirt. Jill smiled. The mystery was solved!

Turn the page.

1 **What is the big idea in this story?**

- ○ It is fun to solve a mystery.
- ○ Kids like to make new friends.
- ○ People need to work together.

2 **How are Jill and Greg *alike*?**

- ○ They like shopping.
- ○ They have on rings.
- ○ They are detectives.

3 **How is Jill *not like* Greg?**

- ○ She looks for a ring.
- ○ She looks for a painting.
- ○ She looks in a shop.

4 **What is something that Greg and Jill do *alike*?**

____

____

____

____

____

Name _______________________________

Read the selection. Then answer the questions that follow.

Two Friends

Hummingbird felt sad. She wished she could spend more time with her pal Beaver. Beaver lived under a dam in the stream.

"Beaver, will you take me for a ride on your back?" asked Hummingbird. She liked to hang onto Beaver's dark fur and float on the stream.

Beaver liked Hummingbird's light, bright feathers. Hummingbird was so tiny that Beaver did not feel her sitting on his back.

When they got out of the water, Beaver went into the trees. Hummingbird stayed by his side so they could chat. Her wings went so fast they hummed! They had a lot of fun, and Hummingbird had a happy day after all.

Turn the page.

1 **What is the big idea in this story?**

◯ It is fun to ride on a stream.

◯ It is good to have friends.

◯ It is sad to live under a dam.

2 **How are Hummingbird and Beaver the *same*?**

◯ They have light feathers on their backs.

◯ They live in the trees by the water.

◯ They like floating down the stream.

3 **How is Hummingbird *not* the same as Beaver?**

◯ Hummingbird can fly.

◯ Hummingbird is an animal.

◯ Hummingbird has fur.

4 **Hummingbird and Beaver are *alike* because both can**

◯ swim.

◯ talk.

◯ fly.

5 **What is a way that Hummingbird and Beaver are *not alike*?**

Name ______________________________

Read the selection. Then answer the questions that follow.

Squirrels

Gail is a gray squirrel. Rod is a red squirrel. Gail and Rod live in trees. Gail and her family sleep in nests. Rod sleeps by himself.

Gail and Rod like to eat. Gail eats nuts, seeds, and bugs. She digs holes to store food. She eats the stored food in winter when it is too icy to find seeds and bugs. Rod eats pine cones and nuts. He hides them in places like stone walls so he has food in winter.

When squirrels are afraid, they tell each other. Gail waves her furry tail. Rod stamps his feet. This lets other squirrels know that they are not safe.

Turn the page.

1 **What is the big idea in this story?**

- ◯ All squirrels do the very same things.
- ◯ Squirrels work hard to keep their food.
- ◯ It is good for red squirrels to stay safe.

2 **How are Gail and Rod the *same*?**

- ◯ They like to sleep alone.
- ◯ They store winter food.
- ◯ They are both gray.

3 **What is one way that Gail is *not like* Rod?**

- ◯ Gail eats bugs.
- ◯ Gail has a tail.
- ◯ Gail lives in trees.

4 **What do Gail and Rod eat that is the *same*?**

____

5 **How is Rod *not like* Gail?**

____

Name _______________________________

Read the selection. Then answer the questions that follow.

Noses and Hoses

Elephants have long trunks. Elephant trunks are noses, but they are much more. Elephant trunks can scratch an itch. Elephants fill their trunks with water and use them like hoses to spray their backs. This way they stay cool and wet. Elephants drink by spraying water into their mouths with their trunks. Trunks can smell and feel. Trunks can be noses and hoses!

Turn the page.

1 **Which sentence *best* tells what this selection is all about?**

○ Elephants use their trunks to drink water.

○ An elephant's trunk can scratch an itch.

○ Elephant trunks can do many things.

2 **What does an elephant use its trunk for?**

○ to smell

○ to see

○ to hear

3 **What is another good name for this selection?**

○ Water Hoses

○ An Elephant's Tool Kit

○ Wet Animals

4 **How is an elephant's trunk *not* the same as a person's nose?**

____

____

____

____

____

____

____

____

Name ________________________________

Read the selection. Then answer the questions that follow.

Keep Your Hands Clean!

It is not fun to get a cold. It is hard to feel good when you get one. Your nose gets all stuffed up, and your head hurts. You may sneeze a lot.

Everyone gets a cold sooner or later. Many colds happen in winter, and this is bad enough. But when you get a cold in summer, it is very bad! The sun is shining brightly, and you are stuck sick in bed. It is not fair! Drink lots of water, and get plenty of rest. You will feel better soon.

The best thing is to not get a cold in the first place. The best way to keep from getting a cold is to keep your hands very clean with lots of soap and water.

Turn the page.

1 This selection is *mostly* about how to handle

    ◯ winter.

    ◯ colds.

    ◯ soap.

2 What is this selection all about?

    ◯ dealing with getting a cold

    ◯ being inside in the summer

    ◯ playing outside in the sun

3 What do you need to do if you have a cold?

    ◯ Drink lots of water.

    ◯ Play in the sun.

    ◯ Go to school.

4 What is the *best* way to keep from getting a cold?

    ◯ Stay in your home.

    ◯ Blow your nose.

    ◯ Wash your hands.

5 Why is it harder to have a cold in the summer than in the winter?

____

____

____

____

____

Name _______________________________

Read the selection. Then answer the questions that follow.

How Skunks Stay Safe

Skunks have a spray called musk that smells very bad. Skunks spray musk to chase away enemies. Skunks spray when they are scared.

Skunks give warnings before they spray. They stamp their feet and growl. If the threat comes closer, the skunk raises its tail. The tail's white tip still hangs down. If the skunk's enemy takes one more step, that tip goes up. This is bad news for the enemy! The skunk shoots two jets of spray. It stinks! The enemy runs away fast.

One animal is not scared of the skunk's spray. The Great Horned Owl likes to eat skunks. The owls swoop down on skunks and catch them before they can spray. This is the way they beat skunks.

Turn the page.

Answer the questions below.

1 **What is this selection all about?**

- ○ a dance to scare owls
- ○ a white tail to catch mice
- ○ a spray to keep enemies away

2 **What is skunk spray called?**

- ○ musk
- ○ jets
- ○ feet

3 **How many jets of spray does a skunk shoot at its enemy?**

- ○ one
- ○ two
- ○ three

4 **What would be another good name for this selection?**

____

____

5 **How are the owls *not* the same as other enemies of the skunk?**

____

____

Name ___________________________________

Read the selection. Then answer the questions that follow.

Boy and Frog

A boy sat on a log by a pond. He was having fun fishing by himself when he heard a voice.

The voice was a frog saying, "Hi, Boy. May I speak with you?"

"Not right now," said Boy.

"But I can grant you a wish," said Frog.

"Then I wish you would just let me catch fish by myself!" said Boy.

Turn the page.

1 **What happens *first* in the story?**

  ○ A boy hears a frog.

  ○ A boy gets a wish.

  ○ A boy sits on a log.

2 **What happens *next* in the story?**

  ○ The boy catches a fish.

  ○ A frog talks to the boy.

  ○ A frog makes a wish.

3 **What wish must the frog grant?**

  ○ He must let the boy catch fish.

  ○ He must play catch with the boy.

  ○ He must catch up with the boy.

4 **What happens *last* in the story?**

____

____

____

____

Name _______________________________________

Read the selection. Then answer the questions that follow.

Snow Surprise

Jen woke up one day and saw that lots of snow had fallen. She just sat in bed and looked out her window at it all.

Then she called out, "School must be closed today!" No one called back to her. Jen got up and dressed.

"Mom? Dad? Is school closed today?" asked Jen. There was still no sound. Then Jen looked outside the back door. She saw Mom and Dad playing in the snow. They were making a big, fat snowman! Why weren't they getting ready to go to work?

"Hi!" Jen called. "What are you doing?"

Mom just smiled and tossed a snowball at Dad. Jen put on her coat and mittens. She would help them with that snowman!

Turn the page.

Answer the questions below.

1 **What happens *first* in the story?**

- ○ Mom throws a snowball.
- ○ Jen gets dressed.
- ○ A lot of snow falls.

2 **What happens *after* Jen calls out?**

- ○ Jen hears nothing.
- ○ Jen wakes up.
- ○ Jen sees snow.

3 **What happens in the *middle* of the story?**

- ○ Jen sits up in bed and sees the snow.
- ○ Jen gets ready to go outside and play.
- ○ Jen sees Mom and Dad in the snow.

4 **What does Jen do *after* she sees Mom toss a snowball?**

- ○ She gets out of bed.
- ○ She looks out the door.
- ○ She puts on her coat.

5 **Why does Jen feel happy?**

____

- -

____

____

- -

____

____

- -

____

Name ___________________________

Read the selection. Then answer the questions that follow.

Mother's Day

Tim had big plans for Mom on Mother's Day. He would do nice things for her to show her how much he cared for her. He got up and ran the vacuum cleaner. It slipped out of Tim's hands and hit the wall. It left a small hole, but Tim thought he could fix it. Then he made eggs and toast for Mom. The eggs stuck to the pan and got burned. Then Tim mowed the grass, but he ran over Mom's flowers.

Mom said that Tim gave her much more than she needed. She also said that she loved him for trying to make her Mother's Day a good one. Tim said he would help Mom clean up all her surprises!

Turn the page.

Answer the questions below.

1 **What happened *first* in this story?**

- ○ Tim made big plans.
- ○ Tim surprised Mom.
- ○ Tim mowed the lawn.

2 **What happened right *after* Tim got up?**

- ○ Tim made some eggs.
- ○ Tim vacuumed the rug.
- ○ Tim burned the flowers.

3 **Why did Tim want to surprise his Mom?**

- ○ It was Mom's birthday.
- ○ It was Mother's Day.
- ○ Mom had been sick.

4 **What happened *after* the lawn got mowed?**

____

____

____

____

5 **What happened *last*?**

____

____

____

____

   Fresh Reads   Unit 5 Week 5 A

Name _______________________________

Read the selection. Then answer the questions that follow.

The New Baby

Mom and Dad think Cindy's baby brother is very cute. Cindy isn't sure. She thinks he may be a little bit cute. But he seems to cry so much. When he is sleeping, no one can shout or sing or talk in the house. Cindy loves him very much. But some days she wants to be an only child again!

Turn the page.

Answer the questions below.

1 **What does Cindy learn in the story?**

○ She loves her brother.

○ She likes all babies.

○ She is a good sister.

2 **What is the big idea in this story?**

○ Babies are always fun to have around.

○ All babies are cute.

○ Being a big sister can be hard at first.

3 **What did you learn about people from this story?**

○ Family changes are sometimes hard to handle.

○ Sharing toys with others is always easy.

○ Friendship is a very good thing.

4 **What happens at the *end* of this story?**

____

____

____

____

____

____

Fresh Reads   Unit 5 Week 6 SI

Name _______________________________

Read the selection. Then answer the questions that follow.

Plenty for All

Rabbit came to the water hole to get a drink. Frog and Turtle sat by the dry hole.

"We can not drink," said Frog. "We are out of water!"

Turtle asked, "What will we do?"

Rabbit said, "We can dig down. We will find water when we make the hole deeper and bigger."

So Rabbit and Turtle started digging. It was hot, hard work. But then cool water began to bubble up in the hole. Soon there was plenty of water for all.

Rabbit said, "Frog did not help us dig. He may not take a drink of our water."

"That is silly," said Turtle. "Be kind! If Frog gets no water, he will get sick. His skin will dry out."

Rabbit said, "You are right. It is best to share with all of us."

Turn the page.

- -

1 **What happens at the *beginning* of this story?**

- ◯ Animals dig to find water.
- ◯ Animals come to drink water.
- ◯ Animals find cool water.

2 **What is the big idea in this story?**

- ◯ learning to share
- ◯ digging a hole
- ◯ having some food

3 **What did you learn about friendship from this story?**

- ◯ It is not right to share.
- ◯ Be kind to others.
- ◯ Listen to the turtles.

4 **What would be another good name for this story?**

- ◯ Rabbit Changes His Mind
- ◯ Sharing with Others
- ◯ Frog Digs a Hole

5 **What does Rabbit learn from the story?**

____

- -

____

- -

____

Name ________________________________

Read the selection. Then answer the questions that follow.

Making a New Machine

Tom hoped to be an inventor. He entered a contest for children who wanted to make new things that nobody had ever seen before. Tom decided to make a machine to help children learn to play the piano.

Tom worked on his new machine. He made a piano that lit up when a child played it. The light blinked to show children where to put their fingers to play a song. The lights had to go on and off just right for each song. It was hard work!

At first Tom did not get the machine to work right. But he kept trying. He learned from his mistakes. At last he found out how to make it work. He made the perfect piano to teach children, and he got first prize!

Turn the page.

- -

Answer the questions below.

1 **What is the big idea in this story?**

○ Do not tell lies.

○ Keep on trying.

○ Remember old friends.

2 **What did you learn about Tom from this story?**

○ He likes to play guitar.

○ He does not like hard work.

○ He does not give up.

3 **What does Tom learn in the story?**

○ to use a mistake to do better

○ to stop inventing anything

○ to throw away things that do not work

4 **What happened to Tom at the *end* of the story?**

____

- -

____

____

- -

____

5 **What is another good title for this story?**

____

- -

____

____

- -

____